Perfect
Business
Writing

D0620340

Perfect Business Writing

ALL YOU NEED
TO GET IT RIGHT
FIRST TIME

PETER BARTRAM

C
CENTURY
BUSINESS

First published in Great Britain by
Century Business
An imprint of Random House UK Limited
20 Vauxhall Bridge Road, London SW1V 2SA

Random House Australia (Pty) Limited
20, Alfred Street, Milsons Point, Sydney
New South Wales 2061, Australia

Random House New Zealand Limited
18 Poland Road, Glenfield
Auckland 10, New Zealand

Random House South Africa (Pty)
PO Box 337, Bergvlei, South Africa

Set in Bembo by
SX Composing Ltd., Rayleigh, Essex
Printed and bound in Great Britain by
Cox and Wyman Ltd., Reading, Berks

Brtitish Library Cataloguing in Publication Data
A catalogue record for this book is available from the British
Library.

ISBN 0-7126-5534-4

ABOUT THE AUTHOR

Peter Bartram is a prolific business writer and journalist. He is the author of more than 2,500 feature articles in leading business magazines and newspapers. He has written 12 books, including *The Complete Spokesperson: a workbook for managers who meet the media* (Kogan Page); *How to Write a Press Release* (How to Books Ltd); and *The Groupware Report '93* (Policy Publications).

He has also ghosted book and magazine material for other authors, and has edited ten newspapers and magazines, written newsletters and corporate brochures, drafted speeches for senior executives and produced successful direct mail shots. He has also written a radio play.

He lives with his wife and two children in Brighton.

CONTENTS

A CURE FOR WRITING PARALYSIS

PUT IT IN WRITING

Do those words strike terror into your heart? The scene is all too familiar. You've had a good idea that could bring more business to your company, cut costs or improve administrative efficiency. You mention it to your boss. He seems to like the idea. Then he utters those dreaded words. Suddenly, the idea that should have helped you make a mark doesn't seem so hot. After all, writing is hard work. Perhaps you try to put your thoughts on paper. But your idea somehow seems less compelling on paper than it did when you first mentioned it. Best forget it after all?

Forget writing and you can forget chances of career advancement. Few people rise high in major organizations without the ability to express themselves well in writing. Civil servants have a phrase for it. He (or she) is 'good' on paper. It means they are able to describe a state of affairs or set out a course of action convincingly in writing. In organizations where decisions and actions must be justified in writing, such a person will excel. And such organizations exist as much in the private as in the public sector.

Why is writing important?

Perhaps writing seems not too important in your job. You spend most of your time meeting customers, managing other staff or in meetings. Yet in almost all jobs, writing will play some role and the ability to write clearly and effectively will help you to perform that job better. Good writing is important both for you and your company.

For you, good writing:

- Helps you to communicate more effectively with other people in your working life.
- Improves your status in the eyes of people who only know you through what you write.
- Advances your career prospects because you are seen by superiors to be effective in advancing your ideas.

For your company, good writing:

- Contributes to business success by improving communication between employees and with customers, suppliers and business partners.
- Creates, along with other factors, a corporate image of the organization.
- Advances the process of planning and decision making by ensuring that all interested people are lucidly informed of relevant facts and opinions.

In the final analysis, the ability to write well will often be a touchstone, a means of judging whether you are worthy of further advancement. Indeed, good writing can even determine whether you get the job in the first place, for plenty of otherwise well qualified job-seekers have been rejected because they submitted poor application letters.

Writing paralysis: the disease

What is it about a blank sheet of paper? It can have the same sort of mesmerizing effect as a snake on a rabbit. You know just what you want to say, but as soon as you reach for your scratch pad and pen your mind goes blank. Somehow, the ideas which were so clear in your mind won't flow smoothly down your arm, through your hand and on to the paper. You have the classic symptom of writing paralysis.

It helps to understand what causes writing paralysis because then it is easier to cure the condition. One reason is not being able to think of anything to say. And if that is the problem, the cure lies in spending more time researching and thinking about what you have to write about.

In most cases, however, you have plenty to say. Instead the main cause of your writing paralysis is trying to think of too many things at the same time. This can best be explained by considering a meeting to discuss the drafting of a report. If the meeting is badly chaired, everybody will start chipping in with their ideas in a haphazard way. Consider some of the points that might be raised:

- Are we going to split the report into sections?
- Should we write it in the first or third person?
- Will we print it on both sides of the paper?
- Should we have a summary at the start?
- Will we include diagrams, charts or tables?
- What recommendations do we want to make?
- Who should we circulate the report to?
- How much technical detail do we need to include?
- Do we want to number the paragraphs?

All these questions – and many others – need consideration but not in the order mentioned. Writing paralysis is too often caused by trying to think about all these issues at the same time, instead of in a structured and logical way. When you suffer from writing paralysis, your brain is like this meeting in which too many unrelated questions are being raised in the wrong order. What you lack is a framework in which to consider your writing task.

Writing paralysis: the cure
The starting point for any business writing task is to consider some fundamental questions. Answer these

questions and you have created a framework in which to approach the writing task.

- Why do I need to write something? Business writing is not recreational. Nor is it intended for entertainment or diversion. All business writing should achieve a purpose. The writing is an act of creation – of a letter, memo, report, statement and so on – which should achieve a result. If you know what result you want to achieve, you will identify the reason for writing. Often the need to write is triggered by somebody else's action:

  - A customer complains.
  - A prospect asks for a quotation.
  - An applicant applies for a job.
  - A manager calls for a report.
  - A colleague requests information.

When this happens, the purpose of your writing task is often clear. In other cases, the task may be more complex and the results you need to achieve less obvious. However, if you start by defining what result you want to achieve, the purpose of your writing task will become much clearer in your mind.

- What is the most appropriate form for my writing? Having defined the purpose of your writing task, you now need to decide the most appropriate format for the document you produce. You could produce your document in a large number of formats. Some of the most common are:

  - Letter
  - Memorandum
  - Report
  - Minute
  - Note
  - Statement

In most cases, the form of the document you produce will be fairly clear from the task. If a manager asks for a report, he expects to see the document in report format, not as a long letter. But perhaps the manager just calls for information about a specific topic. Should you send it in a letter, memo or report? You need to consider the scope of the task. You must decide how much information you need to provide in order to achieve the result you want.

Take the case of the customer complaint. Perhaps the customer has a simple moan, such as late delivery. You can handle this task with a letter setting out the reasons for the late delivery, what you are doing to prevent it happening again and, finally, apologizing for the inconvenience caused. At a more complex level, a major customer might be complaining about the level of service he has received from your company over a period of time. He catalogues his complaints in detail. In this instance, you might want to send him a report on all the issues he raises, adding your perspective, and describing the measures you are taking to improve service to him. You would send the report with a shorter covering letter.

The lesson: if you decide at the outset the form that your document should take, you will have cleared one of the big decisions about it out of the way. Moreover, because you would write a letter in a completely different way from, say, a report, you have solved your concern about how to draft the document.

● Who am I writing to? This question is important because its answer influences the approach and tone of your document. For example, a letter to your boss will be succinct. Your ideas and opinions will be packaged with soothing phrases – 'It is possible . . . I would like to suggest . . .' – designed to make them seem less abrasive. You will not bother with such phrases in a letter to a subordinate. Nor might you be so concerned to write a short letter. Your subordinate's time is of less value than your boss's.

The same approach applies to all your writing. A letter to a complaining customer needs a different tone from a letter to a satisfied customer. A report to a body of technical experts will require a completely different approach from a report on the same subject to a lay audience. The lesson: defining your audience, whether one person or a larger number, will help you decide how to approach your writing task.

- What information do I need to provide? It may seem strange that this is the last rather than the first question. But if you have answered the previous three questions you will have already created a framework in which it is easier to decide on the information to include and leave out:

    - You know why you have to write the document – so the purpose is clear in your mind.
    - You know the form your document will take – letter, memo, report, etc – which helps you understand the level and detail of information you need to provide.
    - You know who is to read the document – so you can judge the level at which to pitch your writing and the tone to adopt.

With these points in mind, you can focus on the specific information you need to include in your document. You will find it helpful to answer these questions:

    - What information will the reader expect from this document?

- Do I already have that information?
- If not, where can I get the information?
- How much detail should I include?
- Will I need to explain technical terms or does the reader already understand them?
- Out of all the information I provide, what are the key points to stress?

One final point: do not fear writing paralysis or feel you are the only sufferer. All writers suffer from it from time to time. What is important is knowing how to cure it when it strikes. Having a clear framework – summarized in the four main questions above – provides a way of breaking through the block. Soon your words will be flowing on to paper.

Document benchmarks

As we have seen, getting started is half the battle, but knowing the standards you ought to aim for is also important. Over the past few years, business has spent millions of pounds in 'total quality' campaigns. But, too often, one of the most important elements of business is ignored in the quality drive – the standard of the written word. Just how do you assess the 'quality' of a letter? How do you determine the excellence of a report? Does it all come down to a subjective opinion or are there any benchmarks to guide you? When you write in business, just what standards should you aim for?

Here are six:

- Clear purpose. Whatever the document, it should be clear from the top of the first page what its purpose is. When the recipient asks the question 'why have I received this document?' the answer should be immediately obvious.
- Complete. The document should contain all the information the reader could reasonably want. No glaring omissions, but . . .

- Concise. The reader should not feel deluged with detail. You should pitch the document at the right level, bearing in mind the background knowledge of your reader and his position within his organization.
- Accurate. Which means checking facts and proof reading carefully.
- Logically presented. The information should be in the most appropriate order. The document should read clearly. If you are making a case, you should develop your argument from point to point and support it with relevant facts.
- Looks good on the page. There are documents that are inviting to read and documents that repel the reader. Nobody reads business documents for fun, so why make it difficult? Make it easy and become a more successful business writer. Set out the document attractively and woo the recipient to read it.

On all these points, more in subsequent chapters. For now, test the last document you wrote against these six factors. Did it measure up?

A personal writing manifesto.

Is it possible to become a better writer? In most cases, the answer is 'yes', but not without some effort. Most business people will then ask themselves the question, is the effort worth it? Few people deny that training in specialist skills is worthwhile. Managers spend years training to become an accountant, a lawyer, a personnel officer or a production manager. But they too often resent the effort needed to become a better writer. Yet improved writing skills would make them a more effective accountant, lawyer, personnel officer or production manager.

For the manager who wants to become a better business writer, here is a personal manifesto:

- I will invest some time to improve my writing. Start by studying this book and spending some time putting the lessons into practice.
- I will be more constructively critical. Both of the writing I do and the material I read.
- I will ask a close and trusted colleague to help me identify the main weaknesses in my writing. Then I will try to rectify them, if necessary by seeking professional help.
- I will not send out a document I am not completely happy with. I will spend more time to bring it up to the benchmark standards.
- I will make it clear to my staff that effective written communications stimulates efficiency and improves the image of our business. I will help them to develop their own writing improvement programmes.

And finally:

- I will keep the promises I have made in my business writing manifesto.

SIX STEPS TO SUCCESSFUL WRITING

WRITING FOR ACTION

As we have seen, business writing is writing with a purpose. When you write, the aim is to achieve a result. The number of different writing assignments you might have to undertake is potentially huge. For example:

- Report on a budget overspend
- Letter answering customer complaint
- Circular to staff about Christmas holiday arrangements
- Letter of appointment
- Letter of dismissal
- Leaflet about new product
- Statement for the chairman to read at the AGM
- Press release about opening of new branch
- Factory board notice about shopfloor untidiness
- Article about your department for staff newspaper
- Marketing plan for a new product
- Instruction manual on operating new product
- Speech to local chamber of commerce
- Letter handing in your resignation

All these seem completely different. So can there possibly be a common approach? In fact, the same basic approach will serve you well, no matter what the nature of your writing assignment.

The six step approach.

- First, think. Even before you put pen to paper you need to understand what the assignment involves.

You need to ask the four questions designed to clear away writing paralysis. The thinking phase can take a few seconds in the case of a reply to a simple letter. Alternatively, it might take a few days if you have been asked to produce a report on a multi-million pound building project, a detailed marketing proposal or a business plan for launching a new subsidiary. If the assignment is of significant size, you need to divide the thinking phase into a number of sections.

– *The scope of the project.* You need to make sure you understand the scope of the assignment and what is expected at the end of it. In doing this, you may need to ask the person who gave you the assignment some questions. Those questions could include:

• What kind of document do you expect?
• Who will be reading the document?
• What sort of decisions might they want to take on the basis of its contents?
• How much detail would they like to receive?
• When do they want the document delivered?

– *How you will tackle the project.* You need to gain an idea of how you will set about producing and delivering the document within the time available. In order to do this, you need answers to more questions:

• Is the timescale for document delivery realistic?
• How much time will writing the document take?
• Will I need to involve other people in gathering information or writing sections of the document?
• Will other people need to be involved in approving the document before it is delivered?

- How will the document be produced? (For example, will you write by hand and ask a secretary to type it or will you key it straight on to a word processor?)

From this thinking phase, you should develop an outline plan for tackling the assignment. In the case of a simple task, such as replying to a letter, the answers to these questions should fall into place easily. In the case of a longer and more complex task, you may want to write down an outline plan of how you will tackle the task. With your plan clear, you move on to stage two.

- Second, gather information. Except in the simplest of cases, it is unlikely that you will have all the information you need to complete an assignment at your fingertips. Even writing a letter in response to a customer query could involve gathering information from a number of sources – for example, a sales person, the accounts department and a distribution depot. Writing a large document could involve an extensive information gathering exercise.

Information gathering is such an important process in writing that it can make or mar a document. Yet, too often, information gathering gets skimped. The result is the reply to a customer query that doesn't deal with all the points raised (which generates further correspondence). Or inadequate cost data in a report (which causes a meeting to be adjourned pending further enquiries). Or a failure to provide sufficient detail in a sales proposal (which means the business is lost).

The information you gather for a document can be of two types – facts and opinions. The facts are usually the backbone of the document, but the opinions can also be important for they colour the way a reader receives the facts and the conclusion he may draw from them. Facts and opinions are often linked together in the writing of the document. Facts support opinions. (Sometimes, opinions go in search of facts.) Gathering both is not always as easy as it sounds.

- *Facts*: On the face of it, a fact is a fact. Yet life is often not that simple. A fact is only a fact if it is correct. Too often, 'facts' come second, third or even fourth hand. This means that when you are gathering facts for your document, you need to be alive to the reliability of the source that supplies the information. Both people and published sources can let you down. Managers, for example, who seem to be in command of their department, sometimes turn out only to have a hazy idea of some facts.

How can you tell whether information you collect is accurate or not? There are a few danger signs to watch for, and you find those signs in the way people give you the information. In particular, be aware of vagueness:

- I think it is around 20%.
- We have about half a dozen competitors in that market.
- That branch was opened two or three years ago.

In practice, 'around 20%' could mean anything from 10% to 30%, 'half a dozen' could be as many as 10, 'two or three years ago' might be four years ago. Of course, it might be the case that you only need a rough idea. Generalities might be enough, but if you need facts for your documents, they must be precise and accurate and you must make the effort to make them so.

Just because it is in print, doesn't make it a 'fact' either. Of course, some sources are more reliable than others. You would regard a half-year projection of full-year income from your own accounts department as accurate but you might know a newspaper's speculation about that figure to be wide of the mark. Why, then, should you believe the same newspaper's prediction of another company's likely out-turn?

The point about this is that facts need to be gathered thoroughly. There is no need to become paranoid about fact gathering, or to disbelieve everything you read or are told. Instead, you need to apply the qualities of persistence, healthy scepticism and common sense to fact gathering. And if you are not sure about a fact – check. There is little that will undermine your writing more than demonstrably wrong facts.

– *Opinions*. Much business writing involves expressing opinions. Sometimes you will be expressing your own opinions, sometimes other people's. So, often, finding out and understanding other people's opinions will be an important part of the information gathering process. You could find yourself gathering other people's opinions in two main ways.
– *Others' opinions*: In this case, your writing assignment involves you expressing somebody else's opinion. You may already know what that opinion is, or you may have to find out about it in hard and detailed terms. Instances of this include:

● Drafting a note about a discussion by other people.
● Preparing a speech for the chairman.

- Writing a letter for signature by your boss.

- *Your opinions*: In this case, the final views expressed in the document will be yours, but you want them to be influenced by the opinions of others, perhaps colleagues in your organization or outside experts. In this case, you need to understand not only what opinion somebody holds, but why he holds it. Why he holds the opinion will help you to fit it into the context of your own thinking and give weight to it. Examples of working in this way include:

- Finding out market researchers' views on the growth of sales as background for a marketing plan.
- Discovering the opinions of shop-floor staff on the reliability and effectiveness of machinery for a report on improving manufacturing efficiency.
- Asking a supervisor's opinion of the people in his department for a staff assessment.

When gathering information, you need to pay particular attention to collecting information that will support the points you make in what you write. When you have the information to hand, you need to organize it before you start writing, which brings us to step number three.

- Third, plan. Even in the simplest writing task – sending a memo, for example – a moment's planning pays dividends. In a larger writing assignment – producing a report, perhaps – planning is essential before you start to write. In the planning phase, you must decide how the information you need to convey in order to achieve the result you want can best be presented. In other words, you need to work out the overall structure of your document.

In a short document, such as a letter, this may just mean noting the topics you plan to deal with in each paragraph and the order in which you propose to deal with them. For a longer document, you may have to draw up a detailed outline. Drawing up an outline for a report can seem daunting when you have a lot of information to include. So it is useful to have a formula for planning a report. In nine cases out of ten you will be able to draw up a workable outline using not more than three levels of detail:

- *Top level*: These are the main subject areas you will be dealing with in the report, rather akin to the chapters in a book. For example, a report on sales opportunities in Europe, might take the different countries as the main subject areas. A report on moving to a new office might have subject areas dealing with accommodation at the new factory, timetable for the move, resources needed for moving, impact on existing workloads, and so on.

The art of defining these subject areas is to see the big issues you need to deal with in the report. You need to write the subject areas as a list. Leave plenty of space between each item on the paper, so you could add more information to each as you work up your outline in more detail. When you have done so, ask yourself whether everything you need to say can be accommodated within one of the subject areas. If it can, then you have defined all the main subject areas you need for the report. If not, think through the overall structure again, and decide whether you need other main subject headings.

- *Middle level*: Within each subject area, you will need to deal with a number of topics. So once you have defined your subject areas, you need to take each in turn and break it down into topics. A topic is a self-contained piece of information that is essential if the reader is to gain a full understanding of the subject. For example, in the sales opportunities in Europe report, you might have a subject area for Germany and topic areas for West Germany, East Germany and Bavaria. Alternatively, you might divide your report into topic areas for each of your product lines available in the German market.

Similarly, the 'resources needed for moving' subject area of the report on the office move could include topic areas on legal services, removal firms, utilities and services, new stationery, and so on. In each subject area you should make a list of the topics you need to deal with. Again, ask yourself whether you have included everything that a reader will want to know.

Depending on the size of your report, you may feel that planning the subject and topic areas is sufficient. However, in large reports you may want your plan to cover a third level of detail:

–   *Lower level*: Within each topic area, you might want to list the specific information you must include. For example, in the sales report example, under West Germany you might want to refer to your branches in Hamburg, Cologne and Düsseldorf. The utilities section of the office moving report could have paragraphs dealing with electricity, gas and telephones.

Although this may seem fairly obvious, many writers plunge into reports without giving enough thought to the planning. Planning is important because it forces you to think through in detail everything you want to deal with in the report. Moreover, it also makes you think about the best order for dealing with the main subjects, and within subjects with the different topics. This means that you can move the subjects and topics around into a new structure before you start to write the report. If you create such a plan, you should find writing the report easier, partly because you will have thought out the structure in advance and partly because you will have broken down what is a large job into bite-sized chunks.

- Fourth, write. Now comes the task of getting your information down on paper. There are a number of techniques that can help you make the writing easier. As these are dealt with in detail in subsequent chapters, we move on to the next stage.
- Fifth, review. This is a stage which is most often ignored by business writers. At a simple level, it means reading through what you have just written to make sure it says what you want it to say. When reviewing your own writing, you need to check at different levels and answer a number of questions:

  - *Have I dealt with my brief fully*? If you had a written brief, now is the time to re-read it quickly to make sure you have covered all the points. If you are replying to a letter you should glance through it again, to make sure you have answered all the points. A high proportion of written documents fall short of what is needed because they fail to deal with all the issues required of them.
  - *Have I written to achieve the results I want*? At the outset, you should have had a clear idea what you wanted your document to achieve. For example, if you are replying to a customer complaint you want to answer the specific queries

raised, create a situation where the customer continues to do business with you . . . and apologize. In a report, you want to ensure that your recommendations and the information supporting them are clear.

- *Have I written clearly?* You should have written so that your document can easily be read and understood. You should avoid using incoherent or ugly sentences (of which more later).
- *Are there any grammatical, spelling or punctuation errors which need correcting?* (Again, more of these later.)
- *Is the document properly addressed, titled, dated and signed?* Almost all documents have to say where they have come from and to whom they are aimed. Yet sometimes such information is left out.

In some cases, you may find that your document needs to be reviewed by other people before it can be issued. For example, you might have drafted a letter for your boss. In a more complex case, the members of a working party might want to review the draft of a document before it is submitted to the board or a management committee. In instances such as these, it is advisable to produce your document with double-spacing so that the revisers can more easily write in suggested alterations.

- Sixth, revise. Where you are solely responsible for your document, you should make any changes to it as you ask yourself the five questions above. Doing this requires a certain self critical ability. If you start from the position that your work is so wonderful it can never be improved, you will never revise successfully. Samuel Johnson recalled the advice of a college tutor: 'Read over your compositions, and where ever you meet with a passage which you think is particularly fine, strike it out.' That is saying you need to beware of being seduced by your own eloquence.

Sometimes you will have to incorporate other people's suggestions and amendments into your document. You may find that your revisers amend a document exactly, deleting and adding words with precision. In other cases, they write cryptic comments in the margin, often in equally cryptic handwriting. This happens when they want something changed but are too lazy to think of the appropriate form of words to express it as they want it. However, while your colleagues can expect you to be a good writer, they cannot expect you to be a mind reader. So if your document needs to be reviewed by others, it is a good idea to ask them to make any precise changes they want to the manuscript, rather than general comments.

Can these six steps really help you write better business documents? The answer is yes. The six steps provide you with a framework for approaching a writing assignment in a logical and structured way. After completing the six steps you can be more confident you have considered all aspects of your task and produced a document which is fit for its purpose.

KNOW YOUR READER

No business writing is done in a vacuum. It is part of a process of communication which involves transferring information from one person to another. Before you start to write, you need to focus your thoughts on your reader for two main reasons. First, you want to tune what you write as far as possible on to his wavelength of understanding.

Secondly, you want to make what you write as persuasive as possible to your reader. Your document may be aimed at one person, a small group or a large audience of many different types of people. Even when what you write will be read by many people, you still need to give some thought as to the audience you are writing for. You need to hit the target. And that involves understanding what kind of writing will be most acceptable to your reader.

You can understand your reader more by considering two sets of opposites – in and out, up and down.

In and out

The first point to consider is whether you are writing to somebody inside or outside your organization. This is important because it will affect:

- The way you address them. In general, you can write more succinctly to somebody inside your organization than outside (but see **Up and down** below). Some of the verbal massage and communication niceties that you would use for an external communication are not always needed internally. Consider a simple example – replying to a query about whether a particular product is in stock. Internally, you might reply:

Memorandum
Dear George
Thanks for your memo of (date). We have 50 dishwashers left at Ruislip and 20 at Wallsend.
Regards,
Peter.

This is short, brief, friendly, but provides the essential information requested. However, a reply to a customer could run like this:

Letter
Dear Mr Smith (or Fred if you know him well).
Thank you for your letter of (date) about the immediate availability of dishwashers. We currently have 50 machines in stock at our Ruislip warehouse and 20 at Wallsend.
Please let me know if you require any further information.
Yours sincerely,
Peter Jones
Sales Manager.

This is a simple example, but it points out some important differences:

– George only needs a memo, Mr Smith requires a proper topped and tailed letter.
– George's memo keeps the greetings and sign off to a friendly minimum. It also assumes George is fully aware of the subject of his original enquiry. The letter to Mr Smith reminds him of the query.

- The memo and letter assume different levels of knowledge. George knows that Ruislip and Wallsend are warehouses. Mr Smith doesn't.
- Mr Smith's letter invites a further enquiry if needed, to stress the company is keen to provide service.

- The tone you use. The tone of the language you use can be quite different depending on whether you are writing to somebody inside your organization rather than outside. Consider these next two examples, circular letters about the closure of the company car park.

To all staff:

The car park will be closed all day on Monday 5 January for essential repairs and maintenance. Alternative parking is available at the town centre car parks, but staff should note that these tend to become full after 9.30 a.m. The company car park will reopen at 7.00 a.m. on Tuesday 6 January. June Smith (extension 0000) is co-ordinating the operation and can provide more information.

To all customers:

Would you please note that our car park will be closed all day on Monday 5 January? This is so that essential repairs and maintenance can be carried out. Although there is alternative parking available in the town centre car parks, these become full after 9.30 a.m. If you are planning to visit the offices, it may be more convenient if you could arrange your visit on another day. The car park will open again at 7.00 a.m. on Tuesday 6 January. We apologize if these arrangements cause you any inconvenience. If you require

any further information please call June
Smith on (telephone number).

The differences here are clear and crucial:

– The staff memo adopts a succinct tone. All the
 information is included, but it is not dressed up
 with soothing phrases ('it may be more convenient'). The memo is saying: look these are
 the facts and they affect us all.
– The customer memo is phrased in a softer tone.
 The information is presented in a way that
 seems to minimize the impact of the car park
 closure. Unlike the staff memo, it offers a
 specific apology for the inconvenience. The
 customer memo is saying: we have to do this,
 but we will reduce the inconvenience to you as
 much as possible.

• The level of understanding you assume your reader
 has about the subject matter of your communication. This is important because it will influence the
 amount of information you put into your document. A useful way of thinking about this aspect is
 whether your reader has more, less or about the
 same knowledge of the subject matter as you.

 – More: In this case you can use specialized terms
  and concepts confidently knowing that your
  reader will understand them. You should try to
  write in a tone that gently acknowledges your
  lesser knowledge of the subject. This means
  making the document less assertive than if you
  are writing to someone with the same or a lesser
  level of knowledge than you. For example:

  A. In my opinion, the economy will grow
   by four per cent in the next financial year.

B. According to a study by the Institute for Economic Affairs, the economy will grow by four per cent in the next financial year.

In **A**, you are making a dogmatic assertion about the growth of the economy, which might seem arrogant to your reader if you are not a trained economist. Your reader might disagree and wonder about your qualifications for making such a confident statement. In **B** you shift responsibility for the opinion from yourself to somebody else – in this case an undeniably expert body. **B** sounds less assertive. Equally important, if **B** reflects your private opinion, it is a more effective way of putting it across to somebody at a higher level in the corporate hierarchy.

– The same: In this case, you can pitch your communication at a level that you would feel comfortable with if you were the reader instead of the writer. However, it is important to bear in mind that not all people are exactly the same. You may have some areas of special knowledge that your reader lacks, so you should bear in mind the lessons below:

– Less: In this case, the judgement is how much less? How much background knowledge will your reader already have of the subject you are writing about? If you are to write effectively, you must provide enough background information for your reader to understand and make a judgement on the subject matter of your document. For example:

A. The growth of Unix means we should consider porting our own applications to open platforms.

B. The growth in use of the Unix standard
in software means we should consider
moving our own software applications on
to computers which handle the open
systems standards which Unix represent.

To a non–computer literate reader, **A** is a string of
impenetrable jargon. With **B**, more information is
introduced to help the reader understand what is
written. Unix is described as a 'standard in software' and 'open platforms' becomes 'computers
which handle the open systems standards', more
comprehensible even if the reader doesn't know
what open systems standards are. Finally, a jargon
term 'porting' becomes 'moving', which has a plain
English meaning.

• The vocabulary you use. In the end, your document
comes down to words. Will your reader understand
the words you use? This question is related to the
level of understanding and, again, requires careful
thought and fine judgement. For example, all the
borrowers of a building society could be expected
to understand the meaning of the word 'mortgage'
but perhaps not the term 'endowment mortgage'.
Except that most holders of endowment mortgages
would understand the term.

The test to apply is whether your reader is likely to
have had personal experience of the vocabulary you
are using. You need to ask the question: is it reasonable to assume that my reader will know what this
word means?

Up and down
Now let's consider up and down communications,
which applies mostly to written material within an
organization. This boils down to a simple proposition:

an employee will write to his boss in a different tone from the way his boss writes to him. Yet although the tone of up and down writing is different, much friction is caused in the business world by the failure of managers and staff to appreciate the qualities of effective up and down communications. Let us start with communications that go up the organization. Take this example:

Memorandum from section leader to boss
For the third time this week, the computer network has crashed. It was off the air for three hours and, as a result, 170 orders could not be despatched the same day. If the network continues to crash, I can give no guarantee that we will be able to maintain our same-day despatch policy.

This memo seems to the point. It states the problem and the consequence. It is certainly not wordy or unclear. The problem is that it is just a bit too much to the point. The network crashing is a problem for the boss as well as the section leader and this memo is likely to ruffle his feathers. Moreover, although it may not be the section leader's job to find a solution to the crashing network, the memo is purely negative. The section leader hasn't appreciated some of the diplomatic points of upward communications.

The following approach might have smoothed the boss's feathers and earned some kudos for the section leader:

Memorandum from section leader to boss
The network crash yesterday put our section's computers out of action for three hours. Although we worked until just before the last post was despatched, we still had 170 orders unfulfilled. As you know, these network

> problems are making it difficult for us to
> maintain our same-day despatch policy.
> Although we cannot change the network, there
> are some alterations to working practices that
> would make this section less vulnerable to
> computer down-time . . .

This memo is altogether softer in tone and, equally important, adopts a constructive standpoint. The first memo's subtext is saying to the boss: 'Here is my problem. You do something about it.' The second memo's subtext is saying: "Here is a problem we share. May I suggest some ways of tackling it.' Not only is the second more effective as a piece of communication, it is more likely to result in a solution of the underlying problem.

What lessons do these memos tell us about up-organization communication? There are four main points:

- First, the tone needs to reflect the relative position of the writer and the reader of the communication. It needs to be tactful rather than assertive. It needs to employ massaging phrases such as 'you may not be aware' or 'I'm sure you'll agree'. But there is no need to hark back to Victorian times ('I remain, Sir, your most humble and obedient servant').
- Secondly, the communication should be positive rather than negative. The higher up the organization the more problems the reader will have. The writer scores brownie points by suggesting (not demanding) solutions. (Mrs Thatcher was said to choose her cabinet ministers partly on the basis of people who brought her solutions rather than problems.)
- Thirdly, personal opinions should be presented in a low-key manner. The wise chief executive knows that most staff, no matter how lowly, have useful

ideas to contribute. But he will bristle if a junior
clerk tries to tell him how to run his company.

- Fourthly, the specific facts senior managers need
  should be provided. Too often junior members of
  staff forget that their bosses – and their bosses'
  bosses – are not immersed in the sharp-end detail.
  The boss may miss the significance of what you are
  telling him if it is not supported with relevant detail.
  The detail may alert him to a point he had missed.
  But write as briefly as possible.

Now let us deal with down-organization communication. Consider this memo:

Memorandum from managing director to all staff
From Monday 3 June, the canteen has been
designated a smoke-free zone. All staff will
desist from lighting cigarettes until they are out
of the canteen.

Leaving aside the merits of this potentially contentious
decision, is this the right way to announce it to the staff?
Certainly not. The boss is the boss, but he should not
sound like a Gradgrind. While the employee should be
tactful in his communication with the boss, the boss
should be diplomatic when dealing with staff. The following memo would achieve better results:

Memorandum from managing director to all staff
The no smoking policy will be introduced into
the canteen on Monday 3 June. From this date,
you will be requested not to smoke during meal
breaks for the health and comfort of all diners.
There is, of course, no objection to lighting
cigarettes outside the canteen.

This memo introduces exactly the same policy, but in a

less abrasive way. The phrase 'requested not to smoke' is less likely to make smokers' hackles rise than the curt 'desist from lighting cigarettes'. Nobody doubts that a request from the boss is an order, but they prefer to be asked rather than told. The memo gives a reason for the smoking ban – 'the health and comfort of all diners'. And it tries, at least, to mollify smoking hard-liners by dressing up the existing policy which allows smoking outside the canteen as a concession.

What points does the down-organization communicator need to bear in mind?

- First, to treat the reader with respect. Even though you may be writing a communication to a person of lesser standing in your organization or outside, that fact should not show through in the tone you use.
- Secondly, give reasons for decisions. All people are more likely to accept a decision when they know the reason for it.
- Thirdly, use the language of consensus rather than of command. Orders are for the army (and a few other disciplined services.) They now have little place in for-profit and non-profit organizations that depend for their success on team working.
- Fourthly, make sure your communication is clear. Ambiguity and obscurity will confuse people. They will not be certain what you want them to do. Even worse, persistently confusing communications will undermine their confidence in your leadership role.

In and out, up and down – at the end of the day, it is all about dealing with people effectively. The same kind of skills in human relationships that you would use in personal contact are just as valuable when writing to people.

4

PUTTING ON THE STYLE

THE STRATEGY OF STYLE

There are many aspects to style, some of which concern
the technical use of English. But the most important
concern the *purpose* of style. The central point about
style in business writing is that it is part of getting what
you want. We have already seen that business writing is
about achieving a purpose. Style helps you do that.

You cannot underestimate the importance of style. The
style is likely to have as much influence on your reader
as on what you say. It is a human fact that people are
driven by both their hearts and their heads, in varying
proportions depending on the person. Your style wins
(or repels) their hearts and your facts and arguments
their heads. Don't imagine that a superb presentation of
facts and arguments will overcome major deficiencies
in style. Although people are influenced by style and
content, style makes its impact first. It either clears the
way for the content or it slams the door.

So is there a 'right' style for business writing? Unfortunately not. You must match style to the circumstances of your communication. What is the relation-
ship between the writer and the reader(s)? (See the
previous chapter.) What do you want to achieve with
the communication? What style will best help you
achieve it? In other words the strategy of your business
communication and the style are inextricably mixed.

To understand the point, consider this example. You
are a shopfitter who has equipped a new store for a
client. Now the client is quibbling about a cost over-run
on the contract, which you know was quite reasonable.
If you give the client the requested £3,000 discount, he

will give you a contract to fit his store in the adjacent town. If you refuse, the contract may go to another company, but you might still win it because you know your client was delighted with the quality of your work. Ideally, you would charge the £3,000 and get the new contract, but we do not live in an ideal world. A previous exchange of letters has failed to resolve the problem. It is crunch time.

If you want to be certain of the £3,000 but uncertain of the new contract, the core of your letter could read like this:

A.   We explained the reasons for the cost over-run at the time they occurred and you agreed that there was no alternative if the job was to be finished to the agreed specification. Under the terms of our contract, we have no alternative but to insist on payment of the £3,000 by the due date.

We will, of course, provide a quotation for your new store. In the light of the experience gained on the present contract, we are confident that the problems of cost over-run can be removed in future.

If you want to be hopeful of the £3,000 but certain of the new contract, the core of your letter could read like this:

B.   John Smith, our contracts manager, discussed the reason for these cost over-runs with Mr Brown, your surveyor, on the site at the time the problem occurred. Mr Brown agreed that the extra expenses were reasonable and said he would recommend payment. In the light of the satisfaction you have expressed with the finished job, we hope that you will now be able to pay the additional £3,000.

Mr Smith has already discussed with Mr Brown ways to ensure that no cost over-run occurs in the new contract. We are, of course, delighted that you want us to quote for this contract and the relevant documents will be with you within the next few days.

Both of these letters adopt a style which aims to achieve a given objective. If you have pitched the style right, the subtext of each letter should be clear to the recipient.

Letter **A** is saying: we've discussed this long enough. The facts are quite clear and you agree them. Now we want our money, but we want to stay friends. We will carry out the new contract if you pay the money.

The subtext of letter **B** is this: we discussed the problem with you at every stage and you agreed with the extra payments. We think it is fair that you should pay the money and given the quality we provide, which you'll find it difficult to get elsewhere, it would be in your in-terests to do so. In any event, we'll go ahead with the new contract on an agreed price.

What are the elements of style that signal these different subtexts?

- Tone: on a scale of unfriendly, neutral, friendly, the first letter is neutral/unfriendly. The second letter is neutral/friendly. It is a little warmer in tone, sig-nalled by the phrase 'we hope that you will now be able to pay'. **A** puts it much more bluntly: 'we have no alternative but to insist on payment'.
- Vocabulary: the choice of key words sends signals. In the first letter you have 'explained' the reason for

the cost. In the second, you 'discussed' it. 'Explained' brooks no other point of view, 'discussed' implies a two-way exchange.

- Personalization: the first letter is impersonal. The corporate 'we' is used throughout. In the second, individuals are introduced to give the story a more human face.
- Warmth: In the first letter you will 'provide' a quotation, a cold term. In the second letter, you will be 'delighted' to do so, a much warmer and more enthusiastic approach.

What conclusions can we draw from this exploration of the strategy of style?

First, style is intimately interwoven with what you want to achieve. Style is much more than a way of putting a literary gloss on your business writing. You use style as a weapon to get what you want.

Secondly, the style changes the character and the nature of the message. You use style to implant a subtext in your message which reinforces your position to the reader. If you were talking to a person, your body language would give out messages as well as words. In business writing, style takes part of the role of body language.

Thirdly, there are a number of elements – such as tone, vocabulary, personalization and warmth – which can be used to create a style that serves your purpose. You should be aware of them and how to use them to achieve your objectives.

Fourthly, style is a business policy. In the example we have just looked at, the style you choose depends on the result you want. That is a business decision which needs to be taken by those responsible.

Develop your writing styles

You may need to write a wide range of different kinds of communications. You need to adapt your style to suit each kind. Is your writing style set in concrete, or can you match it to the moment? One problem is that too many business people think it is hard enough to develop any writing style, let alone several.

However, it is possible to adopt a more flexible approach to your business writing if you take on board one lesson: writing is a business skill that can be learned like any other. When it comes down to it, the act of writing is about 20% inspiration, 40% technique and 40% persistence. Don't worry too much about the inspiration at this stage – that will come with time. (In fact, you probably have more that you realize.)

Instead, concentrate on the technique and the persistence. In the end, technique boils down to a skill at using the building blocks of writing – words, grammar, punctuation. So you reckon your grammar is poor (you never were very good at parsing sentences at school). No need to worry about that. The kind of skills you need as a business writer are practical not academic. You can acquire them in a similar way to learning a spreadsheet. Indeed, if you have a blind spot about business writing, it may even help to start thinking about writing as using language as a business tool, for that is exactly what you should be doing.

We shall return to the question of technique later in this and subsequent chapters. What about persistence? It is possible for all business people to acquire writing skills, but that does not mean they will use them successfully. Skill is about potential and persistence realizes that potential. No sizeable writing task is ever successfully completed without persistence. First, you need persistence to practise your new found writing skills, to polish and hone them to greater heights. Secondly, you need to apply persistence when you undertake any writing assignment. Persistence means sticking at the job to get it done, not accepting second best, making sure the document you produce is completely fit for purpose, checking, redrafting, refining and polishing until you are satisfied.

Does every writing job require that level of persistence? Possibly not. But every writing task requires some persistence. And a major writing assignment calls for solid application often for very long hours.

Using style as a weapon

We have seen that writing skill is 40% technique. One of the most important techniques is the ability to adapt your writing style to the task in hand. You will find a number of different styles useful to you in business life. One problem in coming to grips with this topic, is that style can be subtly moulded into an infinite number of varieties. However, there are a few common styles which are at the heart of 80 per cent of business writing. So let us explore some of the more commonly used writing styles:

- Leadership style: you use this style when you are the leader and want to convey the fact. Compare these two examples:

  A.   Letter to shareholders from chairman
  The results for the last financial year have just been published and they report an increase in profit of 30%. Despite this, our market is under increasing pressure from foreign competition. As a result of this, it would probably be most unwise to sanction an increase in the level of dividend.

PUTTING ON THE STYLE

B. Letter to shareholders from chairman

I am pleased to report an increase in profit of 30% for the last financial year. But in the year ahead we face increased foreign competition. As a result, I cannot sanction an increase in the level of dividend.

In which version does the chairman sound like a leader? Clearly, **B**. These are the techniques that make him (and can make you) sound like a leader.

– *Write simple sentences.* **B** has three sentences of 16, 10 and 13 words, **A** three sentences of 20, 11 and 20 words, 12 words more than the leader's version. Leaders get straight to the point.
– *Say it hard.* **A** softens the bad news ('our market is under increasing pressure'). **B** puts it on the line ('we face increased foreign competition').
– *Don't qualify.* **A** prevaricates: it would 'probably be most unwise' to increase the dividend. **B** leaves no doubt: 'I cannot sanction an increase . . .'.
– *Display confidence.* 'I am pleased to report . . .' in **B** sounds more positive than the neutral first sentence in **A** which gives no clue as to the chairman's feelings about the results.

You should use the leadership style when you are in a position to make policy, express opinions and set the pace for your organization.

• Soft soap style: you use this style when you want to lower the temperature, keep things calm, avoid stirring up a row. Consider these examples.

A. Memorandum to the Post Room manager

37

I have discovered that you sent the invitations to the sales presentation by second class post. You should know by now that these always go first. Kindly take steps to ensure that this does not happen again.

B.   Memorandum to the Post Room manager

It appears that a batch of invitations to the sales presentation was despatched by second class post. It is established company policy that these should be mailed by first class post. It would be helpful if procedures could be introduced to ensure that company policy is implemented in this respect.

Version **B** sounds a good deal less direct than version **A**, but that is the point. Perhaps the writer has good reasons for not wanting to provoke an argument with the post room manager. The two versions reveal some lessons about the soft soap style:

– *Remove personalities*. The 'I' and the 'you' in the first sentence of version **A** immediately personalize the problem. Version **B** gets round that problem by discussing the problem neutrally in the third person – 'it appears'.
– *Use the passive voice*. Because the passive voice is a more indirect way of writing ('invitations . . . were despatched' in **B**) it sounds less aggressive than the active voice ('you sent the invitations').
– *Don't call your reader a fool*. **A** suggests the post room manager 'should know by now' that sales invitations go out by first class post. He probably does know. It might have been a mistake. **B** states company policy as a means of establishing what should be done in future in a non-

controversial way without pointing the finger
of blame or implying incompetence.

- *Use a longer word.* As a general rule, you should
use a short word when it will do, but short
words can explode like bombs in a sentence
('you sent' in **A** reads like accusation and is one).
'Despatched' in **B** is a softer word and makes
the error seem less of a problem.

- *Don't issue orders.* When you want something
done by somebody who is not in your direct
line of command, make a suggestion rather than
issuing an order. The last sentence of **B** sounds
wordy (and is meant to) but is less likely to irri-
tate the post room manager than the final sentence of **A**.

You should use the soft soap style when you are
writing about controversial or negative issues to an
equal or a superior.

- The 'corporate we' style. This is the organization's
version of the 'royal we'. It is the linguistic equivalent of collective responsibility. Consider these
examples:

   A. I have received an answer to your
   complaint from the despatch
   department. I have contacted them and
   they claim that although your order was
   received on Friday, the following
   Monday was a bank holiday. As they do
   not work on bank holidays, they could
   not send out your order until Tuesday. I
   feel sure they would wish me to pass on
   their apologies for any inconvenience
   caused.

   B. We have examined your complaint. The

reason for the delay was because your order was received on the Friday before a bank holiday Monday. Because the office is closed on bank holidays, it was not possible to despatch your order until Tuesday. We apologize for the delay in sending your order.

At first reading, **A** sounds an acceptable reply. But is the writer endorsing what the despatch department says, reporting it, or implying criticism of the department? **B** solves that problem. This is a complaint to the company and the company as a whole is accepting responsibility for it. In using the 'corporate we' style:

– *Give a unified view.* Don't report the views of one part of the company as though there may be an alternative. One company, one voice.
– *Speak for the company.* You are not writing with your opinion but providing information about the company's activities or views. Your writing should reflect that, even if your own views differ.
– *Accept responsibility.* In **A** 'they do not work' on bank holidays. In **B** 'we do not'. Even worse, the final apology of **A** shuffles off responsibility in a way likely to damage the standing of the despatch department in the eyes of the customer.

The 'corporate we' style is also useful when you are writing a document which involves incorporating information from one or more other people. It ensures that the document is read as the collective view of the company or department that initiated it rather than the personal opinions of the writer. This is true even for letters signed by individuals.

- Committee-speak style: you use this style when you want to report events and decisions in a completely neutral way. Consider these examples:

  A. Committee minute: Park closing time

  Mrs Jones, who is involved with the local residents' association, had written in to complain about 'nocturnal larrikins' in the park. Apparently, the local youngsters get up to 'all sorts'. Quite a few of the people round the table agreed. Most of us think the problem could be sorted by keeping youngsters out of the park at night.

  B. Committee minute: Park closing time

  The committee had before it a letter from Mrs Jones, the chairperson of the Residents' Association. The letter referred to the nuisance caused to local residents by young people using the park late at night. The committee felt that leaving the park open in the evening could result in it being used for undesirable activities. Accordingly, the committee RECOMMENDS:

  That the park gates be closed from 8.00 p.m. to 7.00 a.m.

Version **A** is certainly more colourful, but **B** is more business-like. Perhaps committee minutes should be more lively, but they are written for two main reasons – to describe the consideration of business and record the passing of decisions and recommendations. In using the committee-speak style you should:

- *Speak for the body rather than the individuals.* You are reporting the considerations of a corporate body (in this case, a committee, but in other instances, a working party, planning group, etc.) Your writing should reflect the views of the group as a whole, except where individuals' views are especially reported.
- *Write impersonally.* Refer to yourself and your colleagues only as a corporate body or individually in the third person. You do not want your readers to be diverted by your differences of opinion, but by the conclusions your group as a whole has reached.
- *Be precise.* **A** talks about a letter received from Mrs Jones, who is 'involved with' the local residents' association. **B** makes it clear she is the chairperson.
- *Spell out what action you want.* **A** talks vaguely about keeping youngsters 'out of the park at night'. **B** makes a concrete recommendation. It separates the recommendation from the rest of the text to focus readers' attention on it.

You should use this style for working party reports, committee minutes, and any other document conveying information to an audience of people where the writer's personal opinions should not be apparent to the readers.

- Colourful style. Just as there are cases when you need to keep your style flat and neutral, there are others when you want to make it colourful and lively. Look at these two examples:

   A. **Invitation to an opening**
   An invitation is extended to attend the official opening of the Furniture Happy Mart on Thursday 2 May at which the

ceremony is to be performed by Mr Thomas Tickle, the television personality. After the ceremony, it will be possible to view the products available in the store. Refreshments will be served.

B.   Invitation to an opening

Please, please come to our mega–opening ceremony. The venue: the new Furniture Happy Mart. The date: Thursday 2 May. Don't be late. Tommy Tickle, the hilarious compère of TV's top game show, Tickle Your Fancy, will declare the store open . . . in his own inimitable way. There will be champagne and lots of yummy snacks. And plenty of opportunities to buy. Our Mart is an Aladdin's cave of luxury three piece suites at unbeatable prices.

In version **A**, the opening sounds about as much fun as a funeral. Indeed, the invitation is couched in terms almost designed to put you off attending. **B** makes the opening sound as though it might be fun. So lessons for the colourful style are:

–   *Keep sentences and words short.* Short sentences make for livelier writing. While there are many opportunities for using a long sentence, such a method of writing requires the reader's close attention, and can impede understanding by forcing the reader to disentangle the different ideas from one sentence, a problem he might not have had if those ideas had been expressed in several sentences. See?

–   *Use words which grab attention.* Mega–opening might not be the Queen's English but it wins the reader's attention in the first sentence of **B**.

- *Use more adjectives.* Adjectives are describing words. They add excitement to the ideas expressed. So the compère is 'hilarious' and the snacks are 'yummy'. But don't go too overboard with adjectives. Otherwise, the pace of your writing will slow down and begin to sound tedious.
- *Use a metaphor.* A metaphor is when you say something is something else. In **B**: 'Our Mart is an Aladdin's Cave . . . ' Or you could make it a simile, by saying that something is like something else: 'Our Mart is like an Aladdin's Cave . . .'
- *Be specific.* Saying exactly what you mean always sounds more interesting than a generalization. 'Champagne and yummy snacks' sounds much more appealing than 'refreshments will be served'.

If you can master the strategy of style you will find that your writing makes a quantum leap in effectiveness. It seems obvious that you should adapt your style to the circumstances. Yet there are other factors which influence business writing style . . . often not for the best.

5

TACTICS FOR EFFECTIVE WRITING

WHY AM I WRITING THIS RUBBISH?

George Orwell wrote a celebrated essay on language and politics. In it, he pointed out that the way we use language is increasingly influenced by what we believe – in fact, by politics. Because business is also deeply influenced by management or office politics, the same kinds of problems that Orwell originally identified now afflict much business writing.

Examples are not hard to find. An organization doesn't become smaller but is 'down-sized'. It doesn't sub-contract, it 'outsources'. Workers are not told they're sacked. Instead, they're given 'positive counselling prior to outplacement'. It is very easy, from a writer's point of view, to say that this kind of language should not be used in business writing. Such language is not always used out of laziness, lack of skill or because the writer does not know better. On the contrary, he often knows only too well the dangers of using plain speaking to describe potentially explosive situations. Instead, the language is used deliberately to soften a blow, obscure an unpleasant fact, or divert attention from a damaging situation.

Does this mean the use of plain English is dead in business writing? Not necessarily. First, there are plenty of opportunities in business writing where 'politics' does not intrude. There is no excuse for not writing in plain English in those cases. The trouble is that the weavers of political business English set a bad example. Their obscurantist vocabulary and tautological phrasing catches hold. Unless, of course, you make a positive effort to ignore it. So the first lesson is to resist the influence of bad business English.

Secondly, there is the issue of what to do if you feel political pressures in your organization forcing you into using unacceptable business-speak. The first question you should ask yourself is this: is it really necessary for me to write like this? Will using plain English make solving the underlying problem easier or more difficult? Frankly, it is hard to see how using straightforward language can make solving a problem more difficult. Indeed, using plain language can be a necessary pre-condition of communicating the real nature of a problem to those affected by it. 'Political English' is designed to obscure meaning, to camouflage intentions.

The next question to ask is whether your use of language treats your reader with respect. Bluntly, are you using weasel words and phrases because you are trying to get away with something or even put one over on him? If this is your intention, perhaps you should carry on writing the way you do. But you may not retain much respect among other business people.

If it is not your intention, why are you doing it? Perhaps you think it makes you sound more important. 'The year-end fiscal out-turn was commensurate with our fourth quarter budgetary projections', sounds important. It means, 'we made as much money as we predicted three months ago', a more homely mixture of words which is easier to understand. But before you go for the pre-fabricated phrases, ask yourself: which would I rather read? In the end, the user of self-important English is rather like the person who puts on white-tie and tails for a 'come as you are' party. He may think he looks important, but the other guests are laughing at him behind his back.

If you find yourself dropping into the constipated style of the worst of business English, there is one simple question you should ask yourself. Why am I writing this rubbish? If you decide there are overwhelming business reasons for writing 'the negative feed-back detailed in the market research overview from the established customer base necessitates an immediate reappraisal of the short-term manufacturing plan with immediate effect,' you must, regrettably, do so. Otherwise, just write, 'because our customers don't like it, we'd better stop making it.'

The core of good style

If you have eschewed 'political' business English, what other points should you bear in mind in order to improve your business writing? We have already seen that the style you choose varies from one kind of communication to another and is driven by what you are trying to achieve. But beyond the strategy of style, lie a number of tactics:

- Write briefly. Writing and reading are hard work, so why do more of them than necessary? A large number of business documents are longer than they need be. The reason: their authors have not thought out their writing task before starting it. It is all too easy to scribble away and continue scribbling until you have said everything. You will not, however, have said it as succinctly as you might have done. Because it is not succinct, it will be less readable. Because it is less readable, it will be less effective in achieving your purpose.

George Bernard Shaw once ended a letter to a friend: 'I'm sorry this is such a long letter. I didn't have time to write a short one.' Paradoxically, writing short often takes longer than writing long. It also takes more skill. Short writing involves these steps:

1. Think out what you plan to write.
2. Plan how you will write it.
3. Choose the most appropriate format.
4. Make each point succinctly.
5. Read what you have written.
6. Decide how you can make it shorter without losing any essential information.
7. Revise your text.
8. Go back to step 5 and go through steps 6 and 7 again.
9. Complete your document when you are confident it needs no further revision.

The major reason for over-long documents is wrong structure. Because the structure is wrong, information is not necessarily being presented in the most effective order. As a result, the writer is forced into repetitions and digressions. Lesson: right structure is the mother of brevity.

The father of brevity is good sentence construction. The key point here is the construction of the sentence rather than whether the sentence is long or short. On the whole, you may prefer shorter to longer sentences. But a document that reads well varies the length of the sentences. There are three main points to bear in mind about sentence construction:

– *Sentences written in the active voice are shorter and clearer than sentences written in the passive voice.* It is easier to understand what is happening in the active voice. *Active*: 'I sent the report to John' (six words). *Passive*: 'The report was sent by me to John' (eight words).
– *Avoid verbal ballast.* Read a significant number of reports and you will find a lot of words doing no work but making up the volume. The phrases are not hard to spot:

It seems to me . . .
It should be noted that . . .
It is worth making the point that . . .

There are plenty of others. They increase the number of words without adding meaning, so should be avoided.

A special kind of verbal ballast is tautology – saying the same thing twice.

These new low prices are the result of reductions.

New low prices have obviously been reduced.

Finally, there is a rich undergrowth of words that are often used, but rarely need to be.

The factory has moved to the new site precisely because it is more accessible . . .

Precisely? This word is often used for emphasis when no emphasis is needed. The sentence makes its point just as well without 'precisely'.

Your report was really useful . . .

Really? Another word used for padding. Again, the sentence works better without it.

– *Use short words rather than long words.* Long words often sound more important, but they don't always convey meaning as effectively. 'Additional expenditure' sounds grander than 'more spending' and uses nine more letters, but it doesn't say any more. Besides, a sentence made up of short words is often easier to understand than a string of long words. Winston

Churchill may have coined the phrase 'termin-ological inexactitude' for the short word 'lie' but when he wanted a power sentence he chose short words: 'I have nothing to offer but blood, sweat, toil and tears.'

- Write clearly. If you write briefly you will have made an excellent start in your effort to write clearly. It is easier to grasp the main point of a document written in 500 words than one written in a thousand. It also saves the recipient two or three minutes reading time. Writing briefly forces you to be clear, because sentences which obstruct under-standing stand out more clearly in a shorter document.

  One reason why people write at length is that they want to emphasize an issue they regard as import-ant. They think that pouring more words on to the point makes it stand out more. But it is like tipping rubbish on top of a slag heap. The pile becomes bigger, but obscures the view. In other words, length is the enemy of emphasis. Consider these examples:

  A. It cannot be stated too strongly that if the present circumstances are allowed to continue there is no question that the company will fail to make a profit in the current fiscal period.

  B. At present, the company is heading for a loss this financial year.

In **A** the writer has tried to build up the significance of what he is saying with phrases such as 'cannot be stated too strongly' and 'there is no question'. But he only succeeds in delaying the real message from the reader – that the company will make a loss. In **B**, the writer puts the message up-front. It explodes on the page in front of the reader.

Apart from writing briefly, there are other techniques you can use to make your writing as clear as possible.

- Be direct. Don't hedge your sentences around with 'ifs' and 'maybes' which only muddle the reader:

> **A**. It is just possible, providing our components are delivered on time and if there is no exceptional absenteeism in the factory, that we will be able to complete the order on schedule, but there is also the possibility that the production manager will want another order to take precedence.

What is the reader to make of this? Will the order be completed on time or not? A clearer version is **B**.

> **B**. The order will be completed on schedule subject to timely delivery of components and no extra absenteeism. The production manager makes final decisions about work schedules.

It is easier to see what is happening here. The order will be completed on time, depending on three other factors. The reader can see what those factors are and what impact they might have on an on-time order.

A further writing fault which obstructs direct prose is the excessive use of 'qualifiers', words like 'rather', 'pretty' and 'little'. For example:

> It is rather pleasing to report that the pretty

> big effort of the management team ensured the project was a little under budget.

There is a sentence bringing some good news, except that the sentence is weakened by qualifiers. It is much stronger when it reads:

> It is pleasing to report that the big effort of the management team ensured the project was under budget.

As Strunk and White say in *The Elements of Style*, qualifiers are 'the leeches that infest the pond of prose, sucking the blood of words'.

- Be precise. The reader can only understand what you tell him. If you write vaguely he will understand vaguely. There are many ways to be vague, but vagueness comes in two main varieties:

  - *Casual use of words.* Consider this example:

    > Thank you for coming to see me the other day. I would very much like to think in terms of you joining us but I feel we need to get together again to hammer out details.

The unlucky reader of this letter will wonder whether he is or isn't being offered a job. He might also be puzzled about the need to 'get together again'. The following version clears up all the problems.

> Thank you for coming for an interview on 19 September. I would like to offer you the post of secretary with the company. However, before finalizing details of my offer, I would like to have a further meeting with you to discuss salary and employment benefits. I

would be grateful if you could attend another meeting on 27 September at 3.00 p.m. at this office.'

This version is longer, but at least it makes clear what is going on.

—   *Imprecise use of facts.* Consider this example:

I am not happy about the service we are receiving from your company. Several deliveries were late last week and some were also short. We have also had cases of the wrong products being delivered to the wrong depots . . .

Clearly, all is not well. But the unlucky recipient of this letter will not be able to start putting it right, until he knows a little more about what is going on. Certainly, there are facts in the letter – 'several de-liveries were late', 'wrong products were de-livered'. But the facts are not specific enough. What has happened here is that the writer was too lazy to get the information together to write a precise let-ter, thus:

I am not happy about the service we are receiving from the distribution division of your company. Orders numbered B298 and R367, due for delivery on 7 October, were not delivered until 11 October. Furthermore, order R367 was delivered wrongly to the Chigwell depot instead of to Raynes Park.'

This letter provides the facts the recipient needs in order to investigate the complaint. It is more satis-factory for the writer, too. He is more likely to get a prompt and helpful response to his complaint.

- Be unambiguous. The problem with ambiguity is that you think you mean one thing and your reader thinks you mean something else – or is not sure what you mean. Some ambiguity is caused by careless sentence construction. For example:

> You write: 'Could you let me know by the end of the week whether you will be able to deliver our order?'

> You meant: 'Could you let me know whether you will be able to deliver our order by the end of the week?'

Result: no order but a friendly phone call on Friday afternoon to let you know the order will be delivered next week.

The remedy for this problem is to check every sentence for meaning at revision stage (see chapter 8). You might also create ambiguity when you use words in a special way which is not understood by your reader. Every trade and profession has dozens, sometimes hundreds of these words in its own special jargon. For example:

> We have a large ethical business.

To an ordinary reader, this might suggest the company is run to the highest business standards. But if the letter came from a pharmaceutical business, it would indicate the company supplied a lot of drugs available on prescription – 'ethical' has a special meaning to pharmacists.

A final ambiguity problem we should consider is that of word substitution – what writers call the 'elegant variation'. Consider this example:

> The price of our X2000 computer is £500 and the X3000 system is £750. Alternatively, you may prefer the X4000 machine at £900.

Here, the writer has used the elegant variations 'system' and 'machine' instead of computer. Yet nothing is gained by this, except possibly some mystification by the reader. He may wonder whether a 'system' includes extra elements which a 'computer' does not. The message: refer to the same thing by the same word if you wish to avoid ambiguity.

- Be complete. You will leave your reader puzzled if you do not include all the information he needs to understand what you are saying. Here are some examples of incomplete writing:

> All despatch work is handled at our Preston depot.

Problem: there are at least 18 Prestons in the United Kingdom (plus 20 Preston-somethings). The reader does not know which one you mean. Solution: with places or buildings always give enough information to identify it exactly.

> The working party considered the effect of ACT on DCF in the light of the ZBB policy.

Problem: if this is one accountant writing to another, the reader may know that ACT is advance corporation tax, DCF discounted cash flow and ZBB zero base budgeting. Even so, he might need to cudgel his brains unnecessarily to recall the acronyms. A lay reader will be completely baffled. Solution: always write an abbreviation fully the first time it is used, even for readers you think will understand it. Keep writing it out fully if it is a lay reader, but use the acronyms for a reader with the same knowledge as you. Exceptions: those organizations and concepts better known by their initials than their full title such as BBC and VAT.

> There will be a discount for exceeding our minimum order within a month and a further discount for prompt payment.

Problem: the facts are missing. How much is the discount and the minimum order? Solution: a clearer version would read:

> There will be a 5% discount for exceeding an order of £500 within a month and further 2½% discount for payment within 30 days.

Always put in the exact facts so that the reader knows what you mean.

- Be reader friendly. It is possible to obey all the rules mentioned above and yet still produce a piece of writing which the readers finds difficult to digest. Perhaps the reader finds it 'hard work' reading what you have written. Even though you are not writing for entertainment, it pays to write in a way which helps your reader understand what you have to say. In being reader friendly, you need to consider two main points:

  - *Put the emphasis where it counts.* In anything you write, there will be points you want to ram home and information that is subsidiary. You need to give the important points more weight in the way you write. For example:

    > We acknowledge your order arrived late and we have given you a £10 refund.

This is weak partly because the negative information – the late delivery – is first in the sentence and partly because both halves of the sentence, either side of the 'and' have equal weight. A stronger version is:

> We have given you a £10 refund to compensate for late delivery.

There are several reasons why this version works better. The positive news comes first. The sentence is not divided into two halves. The refund is linked more closely in the reader's eye to the late delivery – the words 'to compensate' perform that task. An alternative way of recasting the sentence is:

> Because your order arrived late, we have given you a £10 discount.

In this sentence, the notion of cause and effect is introduced. Cause: late delivery. Effect: £10 discount. Using cause and effect links ideas logically together in the reader's mind and helps him to understand what is happening.

– *Make ideas flow in sequence.* Sometimes writers string information together without considering the way in which one idea links to another. As a result, the reader is left to consider what seem to be a lot of disjointed pieces of information. Consider this example:

> The components were not delivered until Wednesday. The factory started to assemble them on Thursday. The first order was despatched on Monday. The final order will not be sent until the end of the month.

A clear cycle of events is taking place here, but the

writer is not helping the reader to make a judgement about them. The writer has not thought out how the presentation of these ideas can help to achieve his purpose. For example, this could be part of the factory manager's report to the production director. It could read like this:

> Because the components were not delivered until Wednesday, the factory could not start to assemble them until Thursday. As a result, the first order was despatched on Monday but the final order will not be sent until the end of the month.

In this version, ideas are linked together. Cause and effect (see above) is introduced to the first sentence. The phrase 'as a result' links the information in the second sentence to the first. The writer uses the 'but' in the second sentence to colour the production director's view of how the orders are going. However if the factory manager was writing to a customer, he might draft it like this:

> The factory started assembly work on Thursday even though the components were not delivered until Wednesday. Despite this, the first order was despatched on Monday and the final order will be sent by the end of the month.

In this version, the factory manager gives the customer a more positive view of events. The positive news is in the first part of the first sentence. The 'even though' emphasizes how quickly the factory started to assemble the components once it had received them. In the second sentence 'despite this' again emphasizes the positive aspect of delivering the orders despite the difficulties.

Final faults

If you follow the points mentioned here, you will eliminate many of the possible areas of fault in your writing.

There are a few other miscellaneous problems you need to be aware of:

- Clichés. You should avoid clichés like the plague (although this sentence hasn't). Because clichés are tired and second rate their excessive use can give your writing the same flavour. Clichés are a sub-stitute for thought. They can also make the reader feel you don't mean what you write:

  > I have explored every avenue to find the model you need.

  The cliché leaves the reader with the impression that perhaps the writer hasn't bothered.

  > I have telephoned all of our branches to find the model you need.

  That says what the writer has done, sounds sincere and avoids the cliché.

- Slang. Using slang usually reduces your status in the mind of your reader. You may think that slang makes your writing sound informal, even friendly. Too often, it just cheapens what you have to say. For example:

  > Because the budget is spot on I have given the project the thumbs up.

  This simply does not sound right, and the reader may wonder about the judgement of the writer.

  > Because the budget is acceptable, I have asked for the project to proceed.

  This sounds more formal but sets the right kind of

tone for a business communication about an important topic.

Pleasing to the eye

When it comes to business writing, appearances are not deceptive. If you open a document and are faced with page after page of text with hardly a break, it looks boring. It probably is boring. Even more important, the writer has not organized the information in his text to make it appealing to you.

When you write a document – whether a one paragraph letter or a 500-page report – if the words don't look good on the page, your reader starts with a disadvantage. So do you. For it will be that much harder to get your ideas across. That is one reason why it is important to think about the appearance of your document. Creating a satisfying and effective appearance is part of the writing process.

There is another reason. Thinking about the appearance of your document – the physical structure of it – helps you to organize your ideas. If your thoughts pour on to the page in a stream of consciousness, the reader is unlikely to see which are your main points. If you organize your ideas visually on the page, the reader can immediately see what you are saying.

Power of the paragraph

At school you may have been taught that a paragraph is a unit of thought, usually with a 'topic sentence' at the start which sums up the subject of the paragraph. This is not a bad starting point for business writing, but it does not go far enough. The paragraph helps you to parcel up your ideas so you can deliver them to your reader one by one.

Another reason for the paragraph is to help your reader

get through the document. The end of a paragraph provides a natural break point in your writing – and in the reading. It is a signal to the reader that you are about to move on to another topic. This means that as far as possible, you should try to follow the 'unit of thought' rule. If you break a paragraph in the middle of an idea, you risk confusing your reader.

What happens if the idea is too big to be written about in one paragraph? Then you have to split it into more than one paragraph. There is no fixed length to a paragraph but if one runs on for, say, more than half a page, it starts to look too long. You will often find that if this happens, you are writing about more than one idea. Look for the natural break points in what you are saying.

A final point: do not underestimate the extra impact you will gain by organizing your document into well thought out paragraphs.

Wide open spaces
After paragraphs the next point to consider is how the words look on the page. There is among some writers a mentality that believes that every part of the page should be filled with writing. Often such documents come from the office Scrooge whose passions in life include not 'wasting' paper and bending paperclips back into shape so they can be re-used. Not wasting paper is a commendable aim, but you *will* waste paper when your document contains words which do not effectively communicate.

Your words will communicate more effectively if you give them room to breath on the page. If you are writing a report–style document some points to consider are these:

● Top and bottom: leave some white space at the top

and bottom of each page. On an A4 page, about one inch at the top and one and a half inches at the bottom is about right. It makes the page seem less heavy to the reader.

- Margins: you should leave reasonable margins at each side of the page – again about one inch is often right. But in some documents where you want each point to stand out, it may be effective to leave even more than one inch.

- Space between paragraphs: in a book, paragraphs usually run on without any space between them. In a business report (and sometimes a letter) it is often more effective to leave a line space between each paragraph. The space helps to give a visual structure to the information. Where this style is used, the first line of a new paragraph is not indented. The line space has already done the visual job the indent would provide. The same style is increasingly favoured for business letters, although many organizations still prefer to run on paragraphs without leaving a line space, but indenting the first line of each.

- Variable indents: indenting some paragraphs more than others provides visual variety. It also helps to create structure in the information. You may find variable indents useful when you are numbering paragraphs (see below). But a word of warning. You should avoid having too many different line width measures in your document – normally not more than three. The aim of variable indenting is to help you improve the clarity of information – for example, by indenting lists or examples – so the indenting structure should be logical and make sense to the reader. If the reader cannot understand why a paragraph is indented, there may be something wrong with your approach.

A question of emphasis

How can you emphasize information in your document? There are a number of devices, but they should be used with care. The main way of delivering emphasis is in the style you use to write. Typographical emphases should not be used as a fig leaf to cover poor writing.

Another danger is that emphasis methods are used too often, which reduces their impact, or that too many different kinds of emphasis are used close to one another, which confuses the reader. These points are illustrated in what follows:

Methods of emphasis include:

- Capital letters. Normally capitals should be restricted to the start of a sentence or proper nouns. Capitals can add emphasis when used with restraint. The main use for capitals is in headings. They rarely work well in the body of the text of a document.

  A common misuse of capitals is in company and product names. You may think you ram home your company name by always mentioning it in capitals:

    I am writing with details of products
    provided by ACME SERVICES LTD.

  This is just about acceptable, but looks slightly amateurish. To the reader, the capitals look like the typographical equivalent of an inferiority complex. The following works better:

    I am writing with details of products
    provided by Acme Services Ltd.

- Underlining. This is an effective way of giving emphasis to some words and phrases – but do not use it too often. The correct use of underlining is:

  - *Headings*: to give the heading extra weight on the page.
  - *Titles and names*: underlining can be used as a replacement for italics to pick out book or report titles or the names of ships, etc. For example:

    A. The Economy of Europe was out of stock, but I am including the Economy of America and the report Sales of Machinery in South America 1985–1990 with this letter.

    B. The <u>Economy of Europe</u> was out of stock, but I am including <u>The Economy of America</u> and the report <u>Sales of Machinery in South America 1985–1990</u> with this letter.

  In these two examples, **B** is much clearer than **A** because the underlining separates the titles from the rest of the words in the sentence. An even better choice is to put the titles into italics, but you need a word processor that can output different type fonts to do that.

Headline news

One way to help readers find their way through a document is through the skilful use of headings. You will find them particularly useful in a report, but could also use them in a letter. For example, a customer writes asking about progress on three separate orders. You will set out the information he needs in three main paragraphs. If you give each of the paragraphs a heading, your customer will be able to see at a glance that you have provided all the information he needs.

There are two main kinds of headings – those which deal with subject matter and those which describe the structure of the document. Headings which describe structure are simple and often one word – for example, introduction, purpose, objectives, summary, recommendations. These headings help your reader to find the different kinds of information he is looking for. For example, he may want to glance quickly at your recommendations before reading the whole document. That is difficult unless he can find them quickly.

Subject headings deal with the content and are often longer. Even though a heading is just a few words, there is still a skill in writing it. Points to consider are:

- Keep the heading brief. Headings are best written in a kind of telegramese. For example:

    A.   A report which examines the impact of the new opening hours on staff working practices.

    This is too long. The reader has to discard too many words to get at the meaning. **B** is better:

    B.   New Opening Hours: Impact on Staff Working

    There is no need to say that it is a report in the title. The reader is intelligent enough to see that.

- Make headings informative. Brevity is important, but not at the expense of information. Consider these examples:

    A.   Summary of the Chancellor's Budget Proposals

    B.   Effect of Budget on Business Plan

Both have the same number of words, but the first is too general to give a clear idea of what the report is really about. The reader might think the report is just a general overview of the Budget. The second heading gives a clearer indication of the scope of the report. The heading describes the report's purpose. The message here is that you should always try to encapsulate the main purpose of the document in the heading.

Numbers that count

When is it useful to use numbered paragraphs in a document – and what rules should you follow? In most cases, you need to use numbers when you are writing a longer document, such as a report. But there is also a case for using numbers in some shorter letters and memoranda.

You can decide when to use numbers by considering the purpose they perform. There are two main purposes. First, they are an attention grabber. The numbers show your reader the points he must consider. Consider this example:

A.   You will get several benefits from our product. It is fully guaranteed for up to a year. We also provide an extended warranty up to five years. On top of that, the product comes in a choice of seven colours. There will be a 10% discount on orders of more than five units.

B.   You will receive four main benefits from our product:

1.   One year's guarantee.
2.   Five year extended warranty.
3.   Choice of seven colours.

4.   10% discount on orders of more than 5 units.

Version **A** provides all the information, but the writer has presented each benefit in a slightly different way. As a result, the reader has to work at understanding what they are. In **B**, the benefits are numbered and clearly identified. The reader can see at a glance what he is getting for his money.

The second purpose of numbering is for reference. This is particularly important for longer reports where it is easier to cite part of a report by the numbers of its paragraphs than by describing their content.

In a simple case, the numbering convention you adopt is as easy as one, two, three. But in some documents, you will find the numbering rather more complex. In choosing a numbering system for a document you have two main choices:

- A mixed numbers and letters system.

  With this approach your main sections are numbered 1,2,3 and so on, paragraphs with a,b,c and sub-paragraphs with Roman numerals – i, ii, iii.

  This approach can be shown in outline in this example:

  1   Greengrocery
      a Vegetables
         i   Potatoes
         ii Carrots
         iii Peas
      b Fruit
         i   Apples
         ii Oranges
         iii Pears

- A decimal numbers system

  With this approach, the main sections are numbered with primary numbers, paragraphs move to the first decimal place and sub-paragraphs to a second decimal place. Using the decimal system, the greengrocery example looks like this:

1.0   Greengrocery
    1.1 Vegetables
        1.1.1 Potatoes
        1.1.2 Carrots
        1.1.3 Peas
    1.2 Fruit
        1.2.1 Apples
        1.2.2 Oranges
        1.2.3 Pears

Both systems have their uses and their protagonists. In some ways the first approach is more user-friendly because the number-letter-number hierarchy is easy to follow. However, it becomes unwieldy if you need to have a large number of paragraphs and sub-paragraphs within each section. Once you reach the second half of the alphabet in paragraphs, you begin to lose track of how many paragraphs there are. The other drawback is the use of Roman numerals which beyond a point become more difficult to follow – did you immediately know that xviii is 18?

The decimal approach has all the severe logic of mathematics behind it – and some of the drawbacks. You can begin to see one of them in the greengrocery example. All those decimal points start to make the non-mathematical mind boggle.

You may also find that it is surprisingly easy to become muddled when you are numbering paragraphs at three different levels. ('Now should that be 5.6.5 or 5.5.6?')

Whichever approach you decide to adopt, you should keep two simple rules in mind. First, be consistent throughout your document. Secondly, have a maximum of three levels to your numbering system as more levels confuse rather than clarify.

Get a little list

Effective business writing means using words in the best format for conveying your meaning. Sometimes you will find that a list or a table can improve the clarity of what you write and save a lot of words as well. Consider the next examples:

A. The branches in Luton, Norwich and Northampton will be closed. The branches in Peterborough, Ipswich, Southend, Faversham and Dover will be expanded. The branches in Oxford, Reading, Slough, Newbury and Gloucester will be reviewed in six months' time.

B. Branch status is as follows:
To be closed:
Luton
Norwich
Northampton
To be expanded:
Peterborough
Ipswich
Southend
Faversham
Dover

> *To be reviewed in six months:*
> Oxford
> Reading
> Slough
> Newbury
> Gloucester

Both **A** and **B** contain the same information, but the list in **B** makes the information clearer on the page. It also removes the need to write three similar boring sentences one after the other.

A list becomes even more useful when it turns into a table, which is essentially a series of co-ordinated lists. Consider this example:

> **A.** Several members of staff will be involved in completing the contract and each will have a timescale. Ted Jones, in the body shop will have to ensure that all units are sprayed. Tom Brown, in warehousing will have to make sure the units are packed. Meg Smith in despatch must send out the order to the customer by 20th May. In order to do this, Tom will have to complete the packing by the 18th which means that Ted must finish the paint spraying by the 14th.

In this paragraph, the three people mentioned must search among the words to find out what they have to do. Now look at an alternative way of presenting the same information:

B. CONTRACT COMPLETION

Department	Task	Responsibility	Deadline
Body Shop	Paint spraying	Ted Jones	May 14
Warehouse	Packing	Tom Brown	May 18
Despatch	Posting	Meg Smith	May 20

This is much clearer. Moreover, because the information is presented logically and clearly, it looks as though the job has been organized sensibly. Every person involved can see at a glance what he or she has to do and by when. Moreover, the tabular approach describes the tasks in a logical sequence which the text version does not.

Tables, such as this, are greatly under-used in business writing. They add value to information for the reader by displaying it more clearly and by showing the relationships between different parts of the information. You will also find that putting information in a table helps you as a writer to establish that you have thought out what you want to say logically and that every piece of information you need to convey is included.

7

SUBJUNCTIVES, SEMICOLONS AND STUFF

GRAMMAR AND COMMON SENSE

It may seem strange to you that a book about business writing should leave grammar almost to the end. Does this mean that grammar is not really important? Certainly not. Grammar is as important to understanding language as driving on the left is to avoiding traffic accidents.

On the other hand, there is no need to become a grammar freak. It is possible to write well without understanding some of the more obscure rules of grammar, just as it is possible to drive a car without understanding what goes on underneath the bonnet. However, there may be a few occasions when you are perplexed about a point, so it does help to understand a few formal rules of grammar. For example, should you write:

A. None of us is able to attend the annual general meeting.

B. None of us are able to attend the annual general meeting.

Which is correct? One school of thought argues that because 'none' is a contraction of 'not one', it must be followed by a singular verb. So **A** is the correct version. On the other hand, that unimpeachable grammatical authority *Fowler's Modern English Usage* explicitly states that it is a 'mistake' to assume that none is singular only. And the *Oxford English Dictionary* says that the plural construction is more common.

See how complex fine points of grammar can become?

You can end up losing sight of the main issue, which is to write clear and persuasive English.

The 'none' example shows that, with grammar, there is not always a 'right' answer. However, in most cases there are. Whoops! That should read 'in most cases there is'. The verb in the sentence is governed by 'answer' which, in this context, is 'understood'.

What you need as a business writer are a few guidelines with which to judge questions of grammar:

- Be kind to the Queen's English. Grammar is an aid to understanding, so it is foolish to ignore it as though it weren't important. Precision is often important in business English and you use grammar to engrave an exact meaning into a sentence.
- Keep a sense of proportion. On the other hand, you do not want to become obsessed by grammar. Grammar is a tool of language, like words and punctuation. A good workman cares for his tools, but recognizes that they are less important than what he makes with them.
- Ignore language superstitions. These include supposed rules which nobody has ever followed, such as never beginning a sentence with 'and' or 'but'. Such superstitions mostly seem to emanate from aging school teachers, who have, themselves, forgotten where they first learnt them.

In any event, good writing is largely a question of having an ear for the language rather than an exhaustive knowledge of the rules of grammar. Perhaps you already have a good ear for English in which case a sentence that is grammatically incorrect will sound wrong:

> Five per cent of the staff could be cut from each branch and yet still be able to handle the same amount of business.

You can just feel something is wrong with that sentence, even if you cannot immediately put your finger on what it is. When a sentence sounds as though it might be wrong, you need to look more closely at its meaning. What does the sentence mean? It is saying that the five per cent of staff cut from the branch (rather than the 95 per cent left) will be able to handle the same amount of business. What it wants to say is that the branch will be able to handle the same amount of business, after a five per cent staff cut. The sentence needs to be recast:

> Each branch could sustain a five per cent staff
> cut and yet still handle the same amount of
> business.

What should you do if you do not have a good ear for language? You must try to develop one. Listen more closely when good English is spoken. Try to grasp the essential simplicity which lies behind the construction of a sentence which is easy to understand. Make a conscious effort to eliminate any common faults you know you have, such as using double negatives – 'we don't need none' instead of 'we don't need any'. In time, perhaps quite quickly, you will find you develop a natural feel for the correct use of English.

Avoiding common mistakes

Even writers with a good grasp of grammar occasionally make a slip. And some slips are more common than others. In business English the worst slips are those which obscure or even change the meaning of what you intended to write. Eight of the most common mistakes in the use of business English are:

- The roving pronoun. When using a pronoun, make sure the reader understands to which noun it refers.

  > Mr Brown has discussed the paperwork with
  > Mr Smith and he will deal with it.

Who is dealing with the paperwork? Is it Mr Brown or Mr Smith? The pronoun 'he' could refer to either of them. If Mr Brown is dealing with the paperwork, the sentence needs to be recast like this:

> Mr Brown has discussed the paperwork with Mr Smith and will deal with it.

If Mr Smith is dealing with the paperwork the sentence should read like this:

> Mr Brown has discussed the paperwork with Mr Smith who will deal with it.

- The disappearing subject. Make sure you remember what the subject of your sentence is, right through to the end, especially if the sentence is a long one.

> The budget report shows sales are falling and has not improved since the beginning of the year.

Here the singular verb 'has' can only refer to the 'budget report'. So the sentence is saying that the budget has not improved since the beginning of the year. What the writer is trying to say is that sales have not improved since the beginning of the year. The verb should be 'have' to agree with 'sales'. The sentence should read:

> The budget report shows sales are falling and have not improved since the beginning of the year.

- Word order confusion. When you write a sentence take care to put the words in the correct order. Writing too hastily or with insufficient thought can result in some embarrassing gaffes:

The managing director was asked to deal with petty theft in the office by the board of directors.

Dear, dear. Here is word order confusion that could lead to a libel writ. It is, hopefully, not the directors who are responsible for petty theft in the office. The sentence should read:

The managing director was asked by the board of directors to deal with petty theft in the office.

- The Is don't have it. I and me commonly cause confusion. I is used when it is the subject of the sentence, me when it is the object. So this is wrong:

Mr Snipe and me will be going to the trade exhibition.

So is this:

The French delegation will meet Mr Snipe and I at the trade exhibition.

In the first sentence, 'me' is part of the subject of the sentence, so you should write:

Mr Snipe and I will be going to the trade exhibition.

In the second, old Snipey and you are the object of the sentence. It should read:

The French delegation will meet Mr Snipe and me at the trade exhibition.

- Sentence fusion. Every sentence should end with a

full stop. The careless writer runs two sentences together separating them by an inadequate comma.

> The committee decided that the next meeting should be held a week later than normal, this was so the chairman could attend after returning from holiday.

As is often the case with sentence fusion, this is nearly one sentence. Dropping the words 'this was' would fuse the two sentences acceptably into one:

> The committee decided the next meeting should be held a week later than normal so the chairman could attend after returning from holiday.

If 'this was' is retained, the sentence needs a full stop after 'normal'.

- **Never the twain.** The opposite of linking together two related but separate sentences, is the grammatically right but stylistically wrong joining together of two different ideas which should never have met between the same full stops.

> The cargo of bananas has arrived from Honduras and the second phase of the office development in Dagenham is well under way.

This incongruity occurs when the writer hasn't thought out in advance what he wants to say or how to say it. Alternatively, the writer is racing along, pouring out information without thought to structure. It causes confusion because the reader is left wondering whether there really is a connection between a cargo of bananas from Honduras and the office development in Dagenham. Both ideas need

separate sentences and probably separate paragraphs.

- Aberrant apostrophes. According to writer Keith
  Waterhouse, who coined the phrase, these are one
  of the curses of today's writers. (There's an apostrophe used correctly – and another). An apostrophe is used correctly to denote the possessive
  (when something belongs to something or somebody else) or to produce a colloquial contraction
  (such as don't for do not). The following sentence
  contains several common examples of aberrant
  apostrophes:

  > The 1990's are the year's in which several
  > businesses will feel the recessions effect on
  > their sales' figures.

  The sentence is also missing an apostrophe. It
  should read:

  > The 1990s are the years in which several
  > businesses will feel the recession's effect on
  > their sales figures.

- Word confusion. Unfortunately, the English language abounds with similar words which are often
  confused for one another. In a worst case, the result
  is a sentence like this:

  > The principle affect of to many enquiries is to
  > make there sales system impractical.

  There are five word confusions in this sentence:

  - 'Principle' (fundamental truth) should be 'prin-
    cipal' (first in importance).
  - 'Affect' (verb meaning 'to produce an effect on')
    should be 'effect' (result or consequence).

- 'To' (preposition meaning 'in the direction of') should be 'too' (adverb meaning 'more than wanted').
- 'There' (adverb meaning 'in or at that place') should be 'their' (possessive pronoun meaning 'belonging to them').
- 'Impractical' (meaning 'not something that can be done') should be 'impracticable' (meaning 'not workable').

So the sentence should read:

> The principal effect of too many enquiries is to make their sales system impracticable.

What can you do if you suffer from word confusion? First, list the words you find confusing side by side – such as affect and effect. Then look up their meaning in the dictionary. Work at understanding the different meanings of each. Finally, practise using them in sentences.

This chapter is called 'Subjunctives, Semicolons and Stuff'. So far, neither subjunctives nor semicolons have been mentioned. Indeed, both are largely becoming relics of grammatical history. Today, the most common everyday English use of the subjunctive is to denote a hypothetical state:

> If I were you.

The subjunctive may also be heard on most football terraces on Saturday afternoons in such expressions as:

> Clear off, ref.

However, in business English, it is not a topic that need detain us for long.

The semicolon, much beloved of eighteenth century novelists, is on the way out, too. It is *not* a slightly stronger version of a comma, and should strictly be used only to separate parallel expressions in the same sentence:

> The delivery of the sub–assemblies on Tuesday morning, three weeks late; the poor service received from your company over the past year; the failure to provide any adequate explanation; all these lead me to conclude we should end our business relationship.

This is the correct use of the semicolon, but in a piece of business English it looks faintly absurd.

Which brings us to the final point. While forms like the subjunctive and semicolon decay, new words and new grammatical forms are born. The English language is a living organism, changing all the time, sometimes for better, sometimes for worse.

8

ANY OTHER BUSINESS

PARETO PENMANSHIP

Picture this scene. A committee or working party is finalizing the draft of a report. Suddenly, a member of the committee fixes on one sentence. It reads:

A study of working practices in the factory revealed that materials waste could be cut by 17%.

'That won't do,' says the committee-man. 'The word "revealed" suggests we were hiding the fact. We should write "showed".'

'A poor choice of word,' says another. 'If we say "demonstrated" it sounds more positive.'

'I disagree,' says a third. 'The best word is "suggested" because we can't be certain it would happen in all parts of the factory.'

An argument ensues. Tempers flare, accusations fly, dictionaries are brandished. Nobody stops to ask whether it really matters what word is used or whether there are more important parts of the report to which the committee should devote its attention.

You have probably encountered situations like this. They demonstrate that in writing, as in many other business activities, the Pareto Principle applies: 80% of your effort should be devoted to what really matters and only 20% to the linguistic spit and polish that makes a piece of writing shine.

So what does really matter? Two things above all:

• Making sure the document serves the purpose for

which it is intended. Before you start to write, you need to ask (as we have seen in chapter one) what the purpose of the document is. It may be a lengthy report on developing a new product or a short letter replying to a simple customer query. Which ever is the case, you should ask yourself four questions:

– Does the document provide all the information the reader will need?
– Is the information presented in a logical way?
– Is the writing clear and unambiguous?
– Is the writing pitched at the correct level for the reader(s)?

● Making sure the document helps you achieve your objectives. In other words, your document has to be persuasive. You should ask yourself six more questions:

– Have I selected the most appropriate facts and marshalled them in the most effective way?
– Should I include any more examples to re-inforce my points?
– Does the structure of the document lead the reader towards the conclusion I want?
– Does my choice of language steer the reader towards the conclusion I want?
– Have I clearly stated the action I want?
– Is there any superfluous material in the document which clouds the main points and could reasonably be excluded?

If the answer to any of these questions is no, your document requires some revision.

Revising with a purpose
To revise a document effectively, you need to go through several stages.

First, read through the document, to get a feel for it as a whole. Did the document give you the message you were trying to impart? If not, why? Is it because the document is too thin in content? Are there important facts or examples missing which ought to be included? Did you spend enough time on gathering together the material you needed to write the document, or do you need to collect more information?

If you find the document is not giving the message you want, or not giving it strongly enough, you need to look closely at the content and structure of the document. One reason may be that the document simply does not contain the hard facts and figures to be convincing. Another is that the facts and figures are included but are not presented in an effective way.

If you find either of these faults, your first priority is to put them right. You may need to redraft the whole document or parts of it. But do not start until you are convinced you understand where the fault lies and how to put it right. Collect all the extra information you need before you start to redraft. Make sure that you have clearly mapped out a structure that will be effective before you start rewriting.

If, however, you are happy with the general message given by the document, you can move on to the next step.

In the second stage of the revision process, you read through the document again more slowly. This time you are looking to make sure that each section hangs together logically and that there are adequate links, where needed, from one section to another. In the second read through you will be asking yourself different kinds of questions. Is the document correctly paragraphed? Are headings and sub-headings used where they can be helpful? Are the sentences of different lengths to vary the pace for the reader? Are there any points where the writing is not clear?

If you discover faults as a result of asking these questions, you should try to put them right as you work through the document. Providing that none of them involve major restructuring, they should not alter the overall flow of your document.

The third and final part of the revision process is a check through for spelling errors, punctuation slips or grammatical solecisms. It is also important to check your document for consistency. For example, do you give distances in miles in one part of the document and kilometres in another? Where a word has alternative spellings (enquiry or inquiry, for example) have you consistently used one throughout?

When you have completed these three revision processes, you can sign off your document, confident that you have done your best.

Advice from the great

Be clear about this: business writing is not about literary writing. It is about effective communication. But all writing is hard work. As Samuel Johnson said: 'What is written without effort is in general read without pleasure.' The Roman poet Horace summed up what you have to achieve in business writing as in any other: 'You will have written exceptionally well if, by the skilful arrangement of your words, you have made an ordinary idea seem original.'

But there are even dangers in good writing, according to the British poet Walter Savage Landor: 'Clear writers, like clear fountains, do not seem so deep as they are; the turbid look the most profound.'

Finally, some elegantly expressed advice from Alexander Pope:

> 'True ease in writing comes from art, not chance,
> As those move easiest who have learn'd to dance.
> 'Tis not enough no harshness gives offence,
> The sound must seem an echo to the sense.'